The Burning Lake
Jonathan Locke Hart
Proverse Hong Kong

In **The Burning Lake**, Jonathan Locke Hart explores in a contemporary context the divine and human comedy, taking his inspiration from Dante, but also making and questioning poetry in a world where light shines "on abandoned tires, industrial/ Junk devoid of allegory" and in a world that is and is not real. This poetry is an exploration of mind, body and soul in an industrial and technological world vastly changed from the tremendous mythological worlds constructed by great poets such as Dante and Shakespeare. The poem moves away from this "sullen industrial waste" and the fires of existential hell through the in-between and purgatorial state to one of hope and light. All this is within and without the contemporary world.

Jonathan Locke Hart is Chair Professor, Creative Writing, Comparative Literature, Theory, and Literature in English and Director, Centre for Creative Writing and Literary Translation and Culture at Shanghai Jiao Tong University. He is also Core Faculty in Comparative Literature at Western University and Life Member, Clare Hall, University of Cambridge. A Fellow of the Royal Society of Canada, he is a poet, writer of other genres, literary scholar and historian who studied at Toronto and Cambridge and has held visiting appointments at Harvard, Cambridge, Princeton, Toronto, the Sorbonne Nouvelle (Paris III) and elsewhere. The author of many articles and over twenty books, he has been writing since he was thirteen, and, for more than thirty years, his poetry has appeared in literary journals, such as *Quarry, Grain, The Antigonish Review, Mattoid* and *Harvard Review*. His books of poetry are *Breath and Dust, Dream China, Dream Salvage, Dreamwork,* and *Musing*. He has collaborated with artists on artists' books like *Darkfire, The Waiting Room* and *Stow*. His poetry has been translated into many languages including French, Chinese, German, Russian, Polish, Romanian, Estonian, Greek, Slovenian and Serbian. In 2016, part of his novel, *Not an Incredible Journey*, will appear in Serbian.

The Burning Lake

ଔ

by

Jonathan Locke Hart

Proverse Hong Kong

The Burning Lake
by Jonathan Locke Hart
Copyright © Jonathan Locke Hart 2016
2nd pbk edition published in Hong Kong by Proverse Hong Kong,
under sole and exclusive right and license, November 2016
ISBN: 978-988-8228-66-9
Available from https://www.createspace.com/6616672

First pbk edition published in Hong Kong by Proverse Hong Kong,
under sole and exclusive right and license, November 2016.
ISBN: 978-988-8228-65-2

Distribution and other enquiries to:
Proverse Hong Kong, P.O. Box 259, Tung Chung Post Office,
Tung Chung, Lantau Island, NT, Hong Kong SAR, China.
Email: proverse@netvigator.com; Web:
www.proversepublishing.com

The right of Jonathan Locke Hart to be identified as the author of
this work and of Gordon Teskey to be identified as the author of
'Preface'
has been asserted by each of them
in accordance with the Copyright, Designs and Patents Act 1988.

Page design, Proverse Hong Kong.
Cover image, 'Ascent', Sean Caulfield.
Cover design, Artist Hong Kong Co.
Back cover author headshot by Yupeng Zhou.

All rights reserved.
No part of this publication may be reproduced, stored in a retrieval system, or transmitted, in any form or by any means, electronic, mechanical, photocopying, recording or otherwise, without the prior written permission of the publisher. The book is sold subject to the condition that it shall not, by way of trade or otherwise, be lent, re-sold, hired out or otherwise circulated without the publisher's prior written consent in any form of binding or cover other than that in which it is published and without a similar condition including this condition being imposed on the subsequent owner or purchaser. Please contact Proverse Hong Kong in writing, to request any and all permissions (including but not restricted to republishing, inclusion in anthologies, translation, reading, performance and use as set pieces in examinations and festivals).

**British Library Cataloguing in Publication Data.
A catalogue record for this book is available
from the British Library.**

To Sean Caulfield and Susan Colberg
co-artists on a related project.

They helped to inspire this book,
which was completed in 2008.

Preface

Jonathan Hart's most recent book of poetry, *Musing* (2011), was entirely sonnets, which is the perfect form for repeated and recursive meditation on the self. A sonnet imitates the rhythm of private thoughts by going off one way and then turning back or to the side, speeding up a little as it races to the close. This thought-world is the usual territory of poets.

In the present work Hart turns to a rarer, more public form of address, one that sees the world feelingly in the nerves and heart while grasping it with the mind, assessing it and finally judging it. This is an exercise in moral and political speech.

Hart employs a verse-form as suitable to this book as the sonnet form was to his previous book: the tercets or *terzine* of Dante. He allows himself latitude with Dante's braided rhymes, but the effect of progressive intricacy is the same. Also, the slightly loose-limbed stride of Dante's hendecasyllabic line is continually echoed in *The Burning Lake*. The three-line stanza is an instrument of *mediation*, of getting from here to there through the difficult middle, a middle that belongs both to where we are and to where we are going. The tercet is an outward-looking form, a natural leader.

Few poets – though they include Eliot, Auden, Lowell, Jorie Graham and A. R. Ammons – venture with such authority to speak for the world. This demands a muse – even if she is "Calliope ... tarted up". What, today, is a muse? She is the deflection of creative power away from its narcissistic center in the self. Narcissism, a disease of poets, is the rapid reflection of light back and forth between two glassy surfaces, the surface of the eye and the surface of a pool, creating the illusion of otherness in the latter and of existence in the former. At the outset of the third section of this poem, entitled 'Light', Hart considers how to spring the light out of the prison of reflection – the sonnet form can be such a prison – so that it can shine towards us and even through us, illuminating all, as in Dante's *Paradiso*.

For the three parts of *The Burning Lake* – 'Fire', 'Between', and 'Light' – are modeled on the greatest effort to seize the world and judge it as a whole: Dante's *Commedia*, made up of the *Inferno*, the *Purgatorio*, and the *Paradiso*. The reader is well advised to review the *Commedia* before tackling *The Burning Lake* because points of reference, often no more than a single word, are frequent in this text. However, one does not get far into the second part of *The Burning Lake*, 'Between', before realizing that in a modern work the gothic, articulated boundaries between Dante's regions cannot be maintained. Dante's devils with their trumpet-like farts, his inverted Simoniacs, and that vicious machine, the great pit of Malebolge, uncannily reappear on the slope of a purgatorial mountain leading up into the sky. It is Hart's deliberate plan to fold over the separate regions in Dante so that all will be polluted by Hell. The crimes perpetrated by the thugs in Hell – notably the destruction of European Jewry and the slaughtering tyrannies of Stalin and others – seep upwards.

The first part, 'Fire', corresponds with our present world, in which we find "new ways to pollute and corrupt". Troy falls again, and the banks of the Tiber are littered with syringes. The mystery of existence lies under a veil of sulphurous smoke.

The second part, 'Between', corresponds with Dante's *Purgatorio*, a vast mountain in the otherwise landless southern hemisphere, with Eden on its top, a vertical span between what we are and what we should be. The souls destined for purification in

Purgatory arrive there in soul ships from the distant northern hemisphere, where they have separated from their bodies. Cato, of all people, a pagan but a champion of liberty, stands guard at the bottom of the mountain. If the souls are not intruders from Hell, Cato sternly orders them to start climbing right away. Hart wonders if any soul that has lived through our history is untainted enough to pass Cato. At one point the direction appears to be inverted when the course up the mountain is made analogous to spiritual history from Jesus to Hobbes – not a purgatorial improvement.

Some of Dante's celestial orienteering devices appear in 'Between'; and Hart has a pleasing habit, caught from Eliot as well as from Dante, of naming the world's rivers. Startlingly, there are unburied bodies here, recalling Dante's likeable Manfred, whose soul is in Purgatory but who left his body on the bank of a river in southern Italy. But here, separation degenerates into confusion and any spiritual refining will have to take place in this world, which is doubtful. The questions Dante's souls ask reappear in a new key: "What makes him shoot / The unarmed boy in the head? / Who counts / The box-cars, cleans out the dead?"

'Light' corresponds with Dante's *Paradiso*, recounting the poet's final "itinerary of the mind into God", to use the phrase of Saint Bonaventure, Dante's governing intellectual presence in the *Paradiso*, exceeding other celebrities, notably Albertus Magnus and Saint Thomas Aquinas. Hart could be commenting on these theologians' modern counterparts, the wildly famous literary theorists, when he says, "The scaffold of ideas comes and goes, rind / Mistaken for pith at the time." The bleeding of Hell reaches by capillary action even to these heights, with references to Goebbels and the Nuremburg trials. But true beatitude is humility, knowing, even if one is Albertus Magnus, that one is utterly unimportant, "a footnote to the universe", if that.

Blessedness is the final and, from our point of view, unacceptable eradication of our pride, which is what we suppose to be the ground of our being. To the proud, Heaven looks remarkably like Hell and Hell looks like Heaven, as it does to Milton's Satan when he rises from the burning lake alluded to in the title of this book.

In the technically virtuosic nineteenth section of 'Light' satirical rhyming couplets are splayed across tercets: "And paradise cannot be / An anticlimax on a rough sea / The music of the spheres awry // In the static of an angry sky." Yes it can, Hart is saying. This mocking of Dante's sublime end projects a dimmer but more penetrating light. Let it shine through.

Gordon Teskey
Harvard University

Author's Introduction

The Burning Lake draws its inspiration from Dante's *Divine Comedy* but is also very much its own work. Its three parts are named in turn, 'Fire', 'Between', and 'Light', to suggest the fire of hell or the *inferno*, the between nature of purgatory or the *purgatorio*, and the light of paradise or the *paradisio*.

The poem was written in 2008 and was inspired by my collaboration with two people — print-maker Sean Caulfield and designer Susan Colberg — on three artists' books, *Darkfire* (2007), *The Waiting Room* (2012) and "The Promised End" (in progress). Sean and Susan provided image and design respectively and I the poetry. The cover image for *The Burning Lake*, 'Ascent', by Sean Caulfield, is a testament to the close relation of this book with these artists' books and I am honoured that Sean provided it.

Originally, I had intended to wait until all three artists' books were out or even for a one-volume edition that brought all three together, before bringing out this book of poetry. But life and circumstances have delayed completion, and so, with the blessing of my co-artists, I publish this sister project now. In fact, it is not unusual for me to put aside completed work for years before publishing it. But it seemed that now was the right time to present this work to readers.

My original title, reflecting the names of the three parts of the poem, was originally "Fire Between Light". But during July 2016, Gillian Bickley, my editor and a poet, suggested that I change the title to make it more accessible to the reader and I ran "The Burning Lake", with its Miltonic echoes, past Gillian and Bronwyn Lea, an Australian poet, and they preferred it to my original. The only reservation I have with this title is that it is from Milton's own fallen world of hell whereas "Fire Between Light" reflects the whole movement of the poem from hell through purgatory to paradise.

Although *The Burning Lake* is related, as said above, to the artists' books *Darkfire*, *The Waiting Room* and the as yet incomplete "The Promised End", these three works of course have the additional visual dimension of images working with the text, whether in a book, art show, or film. (*Darkfire* was the subject of a film, in which the film maker asked the three artists to explain their ideas and contributions and how they had worked together to create the artists' book.)

The artists' books are not bound books but prints and related poems, presented in a large silk box, which can be used in shows in galleries. They contain fewer poems than *The Burning Lake*. *The Burning Lake* was inspired by this collaborative work but became a stand-alone verbal text separate from any image.

In its own way, *The Burning Lake* grapples with large questions – past, present and future – such as politics, violence, the poisoning and destruction of the earth, and the individual life determined but vulnerable in its journey. It combines epic with mock epic, its own kind of serious (but not solemn) comedy, looking back to Homer, Virgil, Spenser, Milton, Dryden, Pope, Eliot, Pound and William Carlos Williams as well as to Dante while looking ahead to both the present and the future. My poem combines memory, presence and prophecy, loss, yearning and revelation in a secular world haunted by the divine and the divine overcome by the secular. The form and content of the poem can be satiric and elegiac, full of sorrow and hope, sometimes oxymoronically, that is both at the same time. Sometimes the rhyme echoes the sense or expresses poetic beauty and sometimes there is a gap between the brutality of this world and the desire for order, lyric and song that the rhyme embodies.

For many years, I had read Dante, so I was delighted when Sean Caulfield proposed to Susan Colberg and me the idea for a project, inspired by Dante, and set in the contemporary world.

The poems I wrote for the collaborative project with Sean and Susan respond to Sean's prints and his notes or thoughts about his encounter with Dante and Dante's relation to the world. *The Burning Lake*, also, is born of our collaboration but has an additional source in my writing and reading of long duration and is quite distinct. My poetry in *The Burning Lake* overlaps with that in our collaborative project, but takes on a different form, using rhyme in ways which can seem archaic and which paradoxically call attention to how much the contemporary world, although built on that past, has moved on.

I suggested the titles for our artists' books to Sean and Susan and they liked them, and I hope *The Burning Lake* is also a title that conveys something to the reader. In *The Burning Lake* I also represent a typology of here and there, past and present.

The Bible as well as the work of Dante, Milton and others from the past inform this poem which is also very much about the contemporary world, its own hells, its liminal, interrupted, and waiting spaces, as well as its promised ends or atonements. The hell, waiting, and promise, which are the subjects of the three parts of this poem are now. This is a work that owes much to Dante and the Christian worldview, with all their richness, but it is also a secular poem dwelling in and on the anxieties and destruction of a world that has lost its way in its own dark wood.

In *The Burning Lake* traditional poetic structure and the ancient structures of belief play with form and rhyme born of modern and contemporary poetry. The archaic and the present meet in a drama of meaning, a suspension of belief and disbelief, in a world in which environmental devastation, tyranny, violence, war and general degradation threaten nature, culture and human survival.

The ethic of reading is an aesthetic act just as the aesthetic of reading is an ethical one. However much we have tried, since the advent of Romanticism and the concept of "art for art's sake", to separate ethics and aesthetics, it remains true, as the ancient Greek philosophers — such as Socrates, Plato and Aristotle — knew, that ethics and aesthetics cannot be separated. Oscar Wilde reversed Aristotle's view of art as a representation of reality, when he said that life imitates art. Both ideas seem to me to be true.

Poetry is of the world but it also supplements the world. It is itself just as mathematics is. Poetry surprises, suggests and can be syntactically difficult and irresolvable. Ambiguity is part of its connotative world and it is a mistake for the poet or the critic to reduce that connotation to denotation, the noumenal to the phenonmenal. Poetry should ravish the world with beauty and truth, however quaint those terms are to those lost in a fallen world, to those living in the deeply troubled contemporary world, in the nature that we are on the verge of destroying and with it ourselves. The Greeks saw the simple without simplifying. Homer and Plato astonish us in distinct ways, notably with the intricacy of their quest for the essence of beauty and truth. Poetry surprises. Even if Socrates and Plato had wished to displace Homer, the power of Homer remained for them and remains for us.

Philosophy and natural philosophy (now called "science") have gained precedence, but still poetry speaks to the mind in words and images that reinvent past, present and future in the temporality of making.

But the making of poetry — and this is also true of *The Burning Lake* — does not end with the making by the poet but is completed in the ear, eye and mind — in the spirit-body — of the reader. Poets and readers animate and make the world live. The acts of writing and reading create an ongoing poem, which is itself, but which also moves in the world. Once the poem is made, the poet becomes just one of the readers.

The Burning Lake may have echoes of the past through image, rhyme, allusion and much else, but it is here and now. You, the reader, continue its never-ending completion.

The collaboration of poet and readers is, to appeal to Edmund Spenser, endless work: "O WHAT an endlesse worke have I in hand,/ To count the seas abundant progeny,/ The fruitfull seede farre passeth those in land, /And also those which wonne in th' azure sky!" (*The Faerie Queene*, Book IV, Canto XII). The poet and reader make countless words count on earth and under the sky, a re-creation.

We are at play in work and work at play. This is not the first crisis in the world — this waste of violence, war and environmental pillage, squander and ruin — but this is a moment of decision when we must decide which way to take in our dark wood. This is a physical and existential question and not one for the mind and spirit alone. All are interwoven. The fire that goes through the between-ness of waiting to arrive at the light might be a flicker on the cave wall, a reflection from the burning lake, or something far different.

Jonathan Locke Hart *The Burning Lake*

This poem calls the reader into the wood and into the quest or journey, and in the epic struggle of words the reader is the hero in a world where heroes seem scarce or impossible no matter how much they are needed. What is real and apparent, impossible or possible, dwells in the movement of the words and of the poem as well as in the hearts and minds of the reader as time goes by and in the human desire in time to arrive at a place beyond time.

Jonathan Locke Hart,
Toronto Reference Library,
15 August 2016

THE BURNING LAKE
TABLE OF CONTENTS

Preface by Gordon Teskey		7
Author's Introduction		11

FIRE

I	Here, lost, in a wood, dark,	23
II	He spoke as he wrote how that city fell,	24
III	The river was dry and they cried	25
IV	Edge, hem, bound the abyss	26
V	We are fated to come and go;	27
VI	The walls close in, the cold wind	28
VII	Only the many myths swirl about	29
VIII	The tyrants starve the people	30
IX	The savage space, the ravaging beauty	31
X	Why is Tiresias called again	32
XI	We live in chemical stews, rusted hulks, a waste	33
XII	He died in a bunker, his death-wish	34
XIII	He died after a pickaxe struck his head	35
XIV	Neither black nor white is this hell:	36
XV	And Troy fell again, the fireflies	37
XVI	We had to dodge syringes by the Tiber	38
XVII	I am not God. I cannot consign	39
XVIII	The fens bred malaria, as if	40
XIX	I do not mean to lie like Sinon	41
XX	Perhaps I am the liar of Amphion	42
XXI	For those who dream of a golden age	43

BETWEEN

I	Although there is no between and decrees	47
II	There is a need for translation,	48
III	The rain washes us, the wind dresses our wounds.	49

IV	Perhaps we have two souls or none. The slope	50
V	They believed in election, but many met	51
VI	The book remains even if limbo is gone	52
VII	Leopards need not paint their skin	53
VIII	And so Manto wandered in the cold	54
IX	Here is a sanctuary for a strange language	56
X	What does prayer do for malediction?	57
XI	Do angels give motion to wind and rain?	59
XII	Who builds paradise from political hopes?	60
XIII	Praise broke the silence. Some climb	61
XIV	And the City of God receded, the words	62
XV	Those who nod at tyrants are caught between	64
XVI	In the revolution of the times a hound	65
XVII	Adore that poet's steps in this junk-yard	66
XVIII	What makes him shoot	67
X1X	The birds turn in the street	68
XX	Where is the sun in Jerusalem?	69
XXI	The horses and the candles now transform	70
XXII	Who can be trusted? My name obscure	71
XXIII	The eagle descends	72
XXIV	Between garden and garden	73
XXV	And what aweful thoughts go through	74
XXVI	And so a light as if on a coast,	75

LIGHT

I	What vision of beatitude eludes	79
II	She sat beyond the teeth of the furrows	80
III	She lectured him on freedom of will	81
IV	Light alters over time: she could see	82
V	See how mental stress tears them. Her eyes fill	83
VI	More light shines on them. Cherubs and seraphs	84

VII	Felix costrutto, Dominus. B Nonsense.	85
VIII	Living light, lucent source, triune radiance	86
IX	They blew her to bits after they shot her	87
X	The light that is most beautiful shines	88
XI	This would be a history of factions	89
XII	What mirror could you gaze on and find	90
XIII	Beware science and theology made	91
XIV	Love from Alpha to Omega, reason, scripture	92
XV	The frost came, the pollen went, time still stuns	93
XVI	A rose is a rose, a rose can be sick	94
XVII	And what might end in this flux?	95
XVIII	She was as the moon on a winter's night	96
XIX	And paradise cannot be	97
XX	How soon has time, that's a good line	98
XXI	We are of our time, blind before the future,	99

Notes   101

FIRE

I

☙

Here, lost, in a wood, dark,
As though I were dead, stuck
In a windless sleep, I stood,

As in a dream or error, no order
Apparent, my mouth dry, I hid
From myself, and did not stir,

Faced what I most feared. The lid
Of trees obscured the sky
And a shade fell over me, a cry

From the brush, a song amid
Bleak despair. And a fire,
Almost smokeless, spread

And shrouded any horizon. The sick
World hides the gate, and I am chid
By my mind, heart, soul.

II

☙

He spoke as he wrote how that city fell,
How some died and others wandered
As though earth were heaven and hell

And grace lay hidden.
                          And then a tumult

Rose up, as if in a dark sea
Suddenly on fire:

Burning flesh, illness and pain
Without end
And anxiety came again and again.

III

☙

The river was dry and they cried
On either side, a wheel of fire
Rising and falling with their lives.

Weary and cruel they cursed
As if they lived in perpetual wrath
And in the clammy sweat of terror.

No one could take me to where
I longed for

                        the panic
The feeling I was born in a waste
Where no joy or life would last.

IV

☙

Edge, hem, bound the abyss
I came to face, original sin
Seeping into my brain-stem, lack and miss

Seize me and turn me
To them, into them, in this wood,
And with each breath the panic spikes.

No poetry could save me. A partial light
Shone on abandoned tires, industrial
Junk devoid of allegory, what might

Have been in a world no less real.
And what is and what might or should
Could not green this place for me.

Not all the lessons of history
Or the wisdom of philosophy
Or the dogma of scholars and votives

Could carry me beyond the smell of lust
And those who betrayed all else
For burning lips that would not rust.

V

☙

We are fated to come and go;
I fell as the dead would fall:
Just one kiss and die, she said.

The mind closes fast and slow,
A cold rain fell, and the dogs all
Howled, their eyes hot and red

And sins deadlier, whatever sin
Now meant. Bare ruined castles
Were canopied trees, the din

Of my heart in silence. My vassal
Soul shook at the word "evil"
And its enacting. And the will

To power, humans contending
World without end, shivered my bones
And the perse oozings of sludge

Ran off in a sullen industrial waste
And the fens stretched out toward damp
And in the fumes I could not taste.

VI

❧

The walls close in, the cold wind
Shakes the trees with sighs, the dark
Gate stays open, the heart is stone

And the sepulchre of this earth
Takes us in solitary death
And some believe all will rise

Gathered in a valley. The cries
For judgement puzzle his disbelief
And all history, feud, strife

Are dragged through hell and back
In hopes of the end of the earth and time
And the ghost of pleasure, the lack

Of the certain, the what if in turn
Of what might be a soul, wounds
And ruins the flesh like earth that burns and burns.

VII

☙

Only the many myths swirl about
No scourge in flesh, no Harpies
Came to me except in nightmares that rout me

And haunt this heart. Violence
Surges in the streets, but this is no roll-call of those
Who hurt: I head into the wood, clothes

Torn, ashes on my face, fires that lance
These boils, and Alexander lost in India
And the scaffolding falls Sahara

Consumed by sand and sea. Law, doctrine,
Judgement, all abstract in time,
Peel away, and his name remains

Unspeakable amid the punishment
Of fire. But those who assault nature
Bleed and bruise us, lead us to rupture.

Yet I would rather restore, lament,
Than judge — as if I could tell —
Rather heal and mend than split and rend.

VIII

☙

The tyrants starve the people
Ogre's breath.
Rallies, ovens, gulags, purges, pogroms,

The traces of blood and stench.
This is the shadow land. The shades of rain
Are not the same.

The residue, the pain, palms
Turned skyward in bafflement
They pray in the herding haste of day.

IX

❧

The savage space, the ravaging beauty
Of her face lift his heart in the waste
And allegorical discourse

Battens his ears, and always the sea
Turns its surf under the moon
And in this dark fire I taste

The empty woe of a world felled
By death. Violence and force
Descend into a river, a blood-rune

As though apocalypse might come.
And from the wold and wheeled
Circles we spin and flicker like Morse

And die and almost die. And so doom
In a catalogue of tyrants, wars,
Strife, reduces us to dust and spore.

X

☙

Why is Tiresias called again
And pity condemned in the face
Of hell? The Etruscan tombs reveal

Punishment and redemption side by side
And all this taken up in Rome, the case
For judgement, with no appeal,

And all those children, women, men
Burning in the mind, launched
In the divine. And the dead bones rise

Cruciform, suffering on the rise, botched
Thorns piercing the bloom of flesh
So much the blood cannot be staunched.

XI

☙

We live in chemical stews, rusted hulks, a waste
Of ancient industry cast and broken,
Graffiti tattooing brick, concrete, any surface

Where it might stick.
                    A token metaphor
Without a harness, a mouth that cannot taste.

                    The dogs bark
As Bruegel paints, the distorted

Features, the tongues rump and roll,
Cry out nonsense against the void. The dark
Boils of night bleed and bruise flesh

And in this pain no bread or grace
Seems near, nothing
Relieves the fear

That takes us. We fall
And sink in scrap and junk
Find new ways to pollute and corrupt.

XII

❦

He died in a bunker, his death-wish
Granted for him and the nation he led
Into madness. The ovens burned to ash

The tabulating machines counting the terror,
Tribal prejudice taking the whole world down
With it. Tyrants across Eurasia

Murdered their own people, and then more
After this earthly apocalypse, and he
Left behind at Aulis. The thugs

Get hold of history: they take doctrine
And make the world a misery
And the roses wilt and burn in a drought

That dries out the stars. Snow is a dream,
A quiet blanket after the killing.
The men, whose tattoos I saw as a child

Seared into their forearms, numbers
Scorched in race-hatred, cry while ersatz myth
Wastes the earth-soul in lashing inferno.

XIII

☙

He died after a pickaxe struck his head
In Mexico while the tyrant lay in his bed
Along the river Pushkin knew, and a corpse

Lay waxed and staid in state, a lapse
Of the revolution, bones broken in blood
In the machine, in the rising flood

Of modernization. Where, in the vestige
Of smoke, in the breath on the ridge,
By the stair that goes nowhere, can they stand

And find peace? Why do they all meddle
With grace and yard where people seek
Their own private lives? This is the dubious battle

Of all those who would wreak
Death with both hands
In the garden we dream and make.

XIV

☙

Neither black nor white is this hell:
Nature buried in concrete,
Rust, waste. In this dry wind who can tell

What more we can do to desecrate?
In this once garden, he punished all sorts,
Named them in sin. Wait,

A thief steals another soul, makes sport
Of the heaviness of furniture. He leaves
The books and takes all else. Snakes

And demons metamorphose, wreathe
And heave in a heap, monsters rise
Up in a tapestry that distorts

Faces, a cartoon of sin, earthly strife
Read revenge in hell. And what lies
Are told, and how partisan, in this afterlife?

XV

And Troy fell again, the fireflies
Flickering over swamp even to Hades,
And the wound, still open, bled

In the enmity of the sons of Oedipus,
A parted fire, vanishing and wistful, red
As dubious battle, and those who would miss

The dead rise up. A vanishing slope
Comes before and after, and genius
Goes astray and with it hope

As those who devise and counsel die
Amidst the right angles of lies. Bliss
For the Lombard was not that for the wry

Florentine. The figures become characters.
And all history – wounds, blood, blisters –
Is one death that begets many.

XVI

☙

We had to dodge syringes by the Tiber
And found them in bins in Saint Kilda's
Around the world. The litter of addiction, the laws

Of oblivion took us in. Hell is not cyber
But what we make. The de Born
Conspiracy divided father and son.

And even the poets who sang of the Khyber
Are silent now. Bards are politics
Even as they cross the River Styx.

Even the shade is mutilated. Time
Lies fractured and speculation haunts
The grim scene made of blood and grime.

Industrial hulks, run-down sheds and huts,
Lean and leak in a land gaunt
With winter, as if greed makes us all sluts.

XVII

☙

I am not God. I cannot consign
Tyrants from Alcibiades to Hitler to hell,
Make ditches and bunkers circles, malign

Those who cast their people in a spell,
Those people in forms and at rallies
Who killed rivals, gypsies and Jews

With grandiose cowardice, their tallies
Kept by bureaucrats and then computers, dues,
Tithes, taxes, expropriations, galleys

Pressing gangs, prisoners, scientists, crews
Into their iniquity. I cannot judge
Being measured in my measure, blues

Waiting, rap, pleas, cries from the sludge
As if humans were nothing. I will not decry
But will record our dark side. Can truth lie?

XVIII

☙

The fens bred malaria, as if
Alchemy could cure it, as though
Bleeding could allay it, the whiff

Of sickness and death stifled them, and low
The moon sat on the shoulder of the mountain,
The tears of Hecuba fell far and slow,

Her children dead. Killed, they eat at her
With each breath. What might have been
Makes her brain race day and night, stir

When calm comes on. And Hamlet is mad
Again. No revenge can assuage pain and loss,
No turning Ovid's book of changes into a sad

Prison where I myself am hell. The cross
Is not about casting your enemies
In textual perdition with you as boss.

XIX

☙

I do not mean to lie like Sinon
I do not call this mirror held up
To nature the glass of Narcissus. No dawn

Can be red as blood. No plate or cup
Can hold the whole mystery. Shame is a leaf.
What kills us can cure us. Go sup

With Achilles. Ask him. Your belief
In Charlemagne lies among the ruins
By the rail that runs between two chief

Rivals in your history. Myth is a rune
As red as my beard. Go with Antaeus
And swear at the gods. And beyond the dune

A nuclear winter waits. The killing machines
Were less terrible then. Lucifer and Judas
Listen to the burnt of Hiroshima scream.

XX

☙

Perhaps I am the liar of Amphion
And make my friends and readers yawn.
Perhaps I let traitors off too lightly

When the heavens do not shine brightly.
Perhaps a traitor betrays in many ways
Reducing sin to doggerel, dying each day

While locked in ice. I come from a cold country
And have suffered several hells, a sea
Of snow buries the lighted wound

As if son kills father at Dover. Doomed
By the white cliffs, blood and snow, the red cross
Is lost at sea. And on D-Day the loss

Was great, the typology as heavy as the sky
And the massacres then and now, the free
Hoping the world is more than a bloody sty.

XXI

❦

For those who dream of a golden age
Stop now. Torture and bigotry have long
Been with us. Feuds and pogroms rage

Then and now. The prison keys and the young
Are thrown into the river. The cages
We build for ourselves endure, the song

Grows heavy with the burden. Their tears
Freeze in the winter night. In quiet rages
They kill their brothers, raise fears

Against their nephews. And the dead
Are dead still. Hold a banquet and slay
Your family. Elysium, tread

Softly in pursuit of nostalgia. Is there
Forgiveness for the errant dead? Clay
We are and dust we shall be. The care

Of inner ice, and three faces, scarlet, black
And yellow, stare out across the waste, the day
Lies stranded on the dark stairs, to a lack

A veil of smoke, the sulphur from pulp,
The sludge from households, the offal,
The negligence, the boredom, world without help,

Leads to a dry zenith, grim and aweful,
Being the nadir, winding, turning, baleful,
Ascending, descending to the light-bearer's tomb.

BETWEEN

I

☙

Although there is no between and decrees
Have killed it, I persist. Calliope
Is tarted up, and black death and other disease

Continue to kill us. The magpies elope, stray
In noise abundant. The four stars elude
These eyes just over the horizon, they weigh

Virtues scorned as quaint. His eyes protrude
As he writes his verse about making the soul
Conform to God's will, and so freedom intrudes.

This might be hard to sell in a time whose goal
Is consumption. Between nothingness not now
The glorious liberty from pole to pole

We seek, through smog, grit, grime and row-house
A peace, natural or divine, that judges and lulls
No one, while computers and televisions glow.

II

☙

There is a need for translation,
Language, culture, study, empire.
Two poets between Aries and Libra shun

The circles between fire and light, pyre
And spectrum. Can a soul achieve
Grace, leave corruption for the lyre,

The song of eternal freedom? You believe
The way between literal and allegorical
Or, when the sign is bent or obscure, bereave.

Loss is loss. Life is as it is. That any decree
Made by a man could order that a corpse
Be tossed from its grave makes dull

The light from the heavens. That, without remorse,
Some play God with armies of the orthodox
And kill the spirit as matter of course.

And nothing resolves itself in paradox
Although prayers and deeds might help
To keep the lion from the fox.

III

☙

The rain washes us, the wind dresses our wounds.
It would be good if life were easy
And lovers could meet under a full moon.

Science gets old too fast. Myth grows lazy.
On the North Sea, the snow
Drives the mind inward. The slow

Deep speech of muthos is a raw
Element in our brain-stem. But the poets keep
Raising theories that cannot explain flaws:

The noumenal tongues and yearnings, the sleep
Poetry wakes from in this dark fire
As if angels with horns sung from the deep.

IV

☙

Perhaps we have two souls or none. The slope
Was high – Alps, Himalayas, Andes, Rockies –
And as we climbed, the sun a mirror of our hope.

We did not care what was left or right. The seas
Could be seen, miraculously, as if from space,
And here microscope and telescope met. Peace

Came over us. And music, full of grace,
Made our hearts glad, as if the spheres
Played on our ears invisibly. This place

Was full of mercy, and all the fears
That accompany life subsided. No stars
Whose fame burned in zodiac and tears

Or tabloids selling the rise and fall: bars,
Clubs, beaches, pools, jets beguile
The rough and tumble of booze, drugs and fast cars.

These should not make the makers all the while
Into gossips, turning life into a tale
De casibus from Adam to the last mile.

V

☙

They believed in election, but many met
Assassination, and this life of blood and flesh
Takes us back to clay and dust. Who begets

Violence? Who still believes, in this mesh
Of time, that wind is the breath of angels?
Yet winds, as they wash over faces, refresh

The spirit, and cool the body's heat. Angles
Acute, right, obtuse, play with eye and mind.
And how does he distinguish between shingles

And pebbles? Those well and ill-born? Find
Those who need to repent? – That's quite a gift.
And the man whose headless corpse fed dogs behind

The church became an icon of the rift
We have with tyranny. Demos is the way
As long as the people do not drift

And become the leviathan tyrant. Say
What you will, poet, even in a nuclear age,
The sage seeks the real, even as he prays.

VI

❧

The book remains even if limbo is gone
Officially. A woman is desired in the distance
A barefoot shadow in white, walking the lawn

At first light. The poet lives an instance
Of exile even at home, a stranger
To himself, and in the pain he winces

And talks about law. People live in danger:
Caesars and bishops are always with us.
He seeks to heal the pagan with the manger

And the cross. What is all this? What fuss
Is made about faith, hope and charity
When we will not feed the poor? The curse

Stays with us in search of grace. Those you see
Who poach, predate, pollute, swindle, torture
Are the flaws we are, so we cannot sing. Flee

Our abject error of making the verdure
Into desert. The rulers fall short, and we must
Imagine, make a world that chases out murder.

VII

☙

Leopards need not paint their skin
Cords will not capture the swimming man
The noose of fraud slips his neck

Invisibly. The reins left a wreck
As Icarus fell, unwaxed, ears blood,
Flesh a pale butter melting that slid

Into the sea in a drop. A fleck
On the surface, then gone, sewn
In a purse. They bury him alive

For simony. Can the damned thrive
And see before? Pride will have
Its fall, at least in the archive

Of poetic justice. His eyes, cruel
And cunning, would not read
Such a book. He would not change his spots.

VIII

☙

And so Manto wandered in the cold
Reflection of the moon. The scratch of claws
On the stones unnerved her. The old

Bridge splintered under the weight of ice
And pitch boiled on the banks of a river
On fire. The bolgia was itching with lice

And the comic chorus of demons, bent
In a dream, broke all laws of laughter,
Leaving the dreamer snorting in terror.

This was a rump trumpet, a chorus sent
To disgust. But the comedy of evil
Left death camps beyond any jest

And made puny any verbal hell.
But here he was, I was, between
Harkening back to ice and fire.

Calliope will sing in this waste
Factories broken by river, canal, road
And virtue is a shattered pole. Haste

Will take these words, make a liar
Of me in careless error. The toad
Turns blue in the pollution. The lean

Wolf hunts in stealth. In the west,
The cloud obscures the light, and the mean
Streak in all souls bleeds to the surface:

Ask Cato whether he can achieve
A soul free from sin, when humans
Are so tuned to God, they believe,

That the quiet of love moves on her lips
And the lake is calm by the snow-cap
And the sun also rises as the moon slips.

IX

☙

Here is a sanctuary for a strange language
The river of salt brings remission
And they who cast no shadow move

And for what sin do they remove
Then occupy the highest ridge
Like soldiers, awaiting a massive army

To strike? The poor man's contumacy,
The hill that rises to heaven by the sea?
They only wander who know grief, unrest

Nimbly playing in heart and mind.
Knowledge is not enough. The desert
Invades the soul. Hitler and Stalin

Both nod by the rail. They wrote poetry
And consigned their enemies to doom.
What was this Cosenza to them?

So many unburied bodies lie
In the wreckage and wrath of history
Under the cold glare of the moon.

X

☙

What does prayer do for malediction?
The shelf of the mountain is sheer, the sun
Is on the left in Rio as it rises,

The wind blows all the way from Jerusalem.
The music rises from the cithern
And the poet sings to the meridian

And those who died by violence moan,
The life of all flesh is blood. Anima.
And all the internecine wars

Cannot people the after-life. Would God
Animate the world with horror and error
Because of the brutality of the human world?

– The roll call of Bormann, Himmler, Mussolini,
The nameless Japanese colonel at Nanjing,
The foot soldiers Las Casas leaves out. –

All nations have their shame: monsters
Dwell within us all. It is what we do with them.
Our hearts are medieval maps, hazards

And wild terrors just beyond on land
And sea. We are all struggling, body,
Mind, soul churning in a death sentence

Not of our choosing. No star or gem
Can shine when our spirits are enshrouded
With cataracts like grape skins. No sense

Is strong enough to resist. We flee
Time at our backs as the sand
Blows in our faces, brittle and round

As an hour-glass. We are cold before
The store that runs out, the chemicals
We spew, the wars we start, this earthly floor.

XI

☙

Do angels give motion to wind and rain?
Lear is mad again, the Fool wags his tongue
In a storm to shake heaven and earth,
The heath is full of demons, wrung

From the mind of Poor Tom. The pain
Of sin plays on the dreaming bones
And from the plethora a dearth
Overtakes him. Can a theology of stain

Make and unmake us? Can it be made
Of such stuff as old kings, and young fools?
Can Siena be turned to Dover Cliff?
He turned to romance with a raid

Of all those who fought for Florence
As if purgatory were a catalogue, school
And jail for friend and foe, the rift
Made universal from circumstance.

XII

☙

Who builds paradise from political hopes?
Parricides, killing even the laws, bury
Athens, obscure grace, taste fate, cut ropes
That bind our exile. Sing of mercy

At Compline. Emperors and Popes
Have slain Italy. Fascism has risen
Again. The widows wear wimples
And eat bitter food. Who rips

The veil? A eulogy not of slumber
But back to the form: it wizens
The soul to inhabit clay

Swallows and nightingales they become
And live between fire and light
That open up music to the dumb.

XIII

☙

Praise broke the silence. Some climb
Up this steep mountain, that pain
Might turn to glory. No rhyme

Could console: time gives rain
And sun, gives and takes away
And in this world of cold disdain

He fell as lightning, lit up the day.
You thirsted for blood and with blood
I fill you, and Troy had fallen on the way:

Arno, Rhine, Thames, Hudson, Yangtze,
Volga, Elbe, Congo, Amazon flood
With corpses, war and the sea

Carrying away mother and brood
And killing the sun on land,
Shadow on face, cast on Holy Rood.

XIV

☙

And the City of God receded, the words
Melting on a hot wind and my book
Was stained, the envious perched

On the second ledge, the letter pricked
From my head. Never travel with rare
Sheets as I did. What vespers took

The pain from my heart. What care
And ruin as the dust coats my tongue
As the mirror of what I might dare

Call heaven, blinds these eyes, sprung
From the dust of the soil. Grace
And mercy take me from rot and dung,

This scrap-heap of history. A face
Raises above this in-between. What light
Can make the hard pace

Bearable? How free is the will, what flight
Can solve the dilemma of time? The soul
Grows impugned as if it were spite,

The cause of evil. And the angry roll
In the blister of high noon, red and white
The heat of that flesh, the bent poles

Of their spines twisted in the light.
Let imagination sing, not of revenge
But on earth as in heaven. Night

Falls like human history. Do not avenge
The slights of angry, lazy men
But embrace love. And at the fringe

We imagine good when
None exists. Let the moon rise
And from the pain

Of earth let heaven open and lies
Be shed and the wilderness be left
Behind. And the myth of Troy never dies

Between fire and light. And bereft
Of peace in the garden, he sings
Of pleasure, women who blind ears, tilt

The earth, plug eyes, burn up in rings
The measure of reason, consume just love, shake
The soul to the dead of bones. The rungs

Of hell we make for ourselves. The lakes
Burning behind, the horizon ahead
Souls cleaving to dust, what makes

These bones gathers them. The only one not dead
In our house, the garden beyond the gate
The dark light gathers about your head.

XV

☙

Those who nod at tyrants are caught between
Ovens and work camps, the violence of nails
The breath of torture, all the obscene

Ways we undo ourselves, boxcars and rails
That make us less human. How can we raise
In the dark corners an evil that pales

Before what it will become? Who plays
At moral failure, turning in neighbour,
Blaming infants as scapegoats? All that flays

We make. The snow was not white, the blur
Of remembrance by the smoke-stack, as the moon
Caught the death of life in soot and ember

Along the winter road. Was it a rune
Or a bigot's sign, a different code
Or alphabet, a world badly out of tune?

XVI

☙

In the revolution of the times a hound
Follows at our back, France is impugned
For seizing the Vicar of Christ, and round

A spiral stair that might lead from the doomed
War of ignorance, they rise and swallow gold
Like Crassus, but some who thirst are groomed

To desire knowledge. And as we grow old,
History never gets old. And Rome is overrun
Once more by earthly power too bold

To be stopped. Not all in this cold, dun
World can be kept, that mountain
Between fire and light now undone.

The wind is not the cause of earthquakes, and sin
And the will find a new way in codicil
While armies fight wars they cannot win.

XVII

☙

Adore that poet's steps in this junk-yard
Or find eternal exile beyond the tree
And thirst is a quest itself. This hard

World chases away life and philosophy
And the prodigal will out and Clio strives
To order time. And on the wine-dark sea

The birth and first-come change our lives
As though they happen in an eclogue. Smell
The stench below, the fragrance ahead, hives

For honey after a long stretch of sulphur. Hell
Hath no fury like locusts or those
Who would judge and might pierce or fell

Their fellows. They hide behind their clothes
While those who hunger and starve and scar
Might fall over when a strong wind blows.

Others feed on the poor and guard their turf
But I cannot judge them, fix them in myth,
While I clean my face in the morning surf.

XVIII

◈

What makes him shoot
The unarmed boy in the head?
What motivates, is the root

Of abuse and killing? Who counts
The box-cars, cleans out the dead
As the bodies pile up, the dying mount

In fields on the outskirts of town?
The smell they ignored, the cult
Of death their sun. What crown

Does the tyrant wear? The tumult
Of his followers left us bare
And wondering: our badges tilt

At right angles to reason. Care
Is an orphan: we wilt
Before those who turn away, dare

Not to know. The silt buries our tongues
Our eyes are pennies, our ears plugged
With silent sirens as we climb.

XIX

❃

The birds turn in the street
Exculpation is far away
The tree of knowledge has no feet

And angels outshine the day
Passive and active the mind goes
This mute tongue cannot play

As it once did. And this rose
Bled from the cross. She does not
Know this man. His heart froze

On the tundra. And in the rot
They fled dogma, left for the deserts
Of Libya, where paradise grows hot

And grace is as clear as the dry air. Spurts
Of inertia freeze this soul, the words
Of troubadours chasing time to the outskirts.

XX

☙

Where is the sun in Jerusalem?
Where is it over Ebro and Ganges?
God, the world has changed!

Atoms, genes, a whole
Microscopic world, a cosmos
Or more, and we are on the shoal:

As time and space change,
We do. And with these changes
We still find Jerusalem

In a cloud. What ranges
Beyond the morning star? Some think,
Others do, and what is strange

About reason? And as we sink
Into oil spill and exhaust stench,
We can try to forge from this rank

World a love. What span or wrench
Can fix a broken heart? Is she there at
The peak? Snow lies on her bench.

XXI

❧

The horses and the candles now transform
To machines and lasers, the moon
Drifts, its halo blends in

The night snow. And soon
Their white clothes become a revelation
And the griffon becomes a rune

That could not be figured. The station
Was surrounded and we could not stop
And our prudence, now of no nation,

Looked back, here and before. Drop
These roses among the lilies. Wars
Are driving us from ourselves. Crop

The picture of pennons now armies, cares
Taking us up. The seven stars
Are sinking their own bloody stairs

As the earth sinks. It stirs
And lilies are in their hands, angels
Singing her before him like a lure.

XXII

☙

Who can be trusted? My name obscure
Will never be mentioned. The snow
Is on the rafters. What can I abjure?

In God we sing a psalm of trust. Slow
These choric voices, forgetful of sin.
And she reproaches him, as visions go,

She could chide him. And in the wind
Her hair blew, and her beauty made
Heaven itself the end of the road.

He wanted to be washed clear, bidden
To be whiter than snow, love and wisdom,
As they sang about her, a raid

On rapture. And he sought in this dome
Her eyes, with Adam at his side,
And truth fallen from his arm.

What harm? And what beckoned, belied
What shone on her, the pole, the glory,
To reach her where no allegory could hide?

XXIII

❦

The eagle descends
Breaks the tree
Strikes the car, ends

By chasing the dragon, the sea
Swallowing up seven heads:
A woman on its horns would flee

Amid the rupture of scarlet reds.
Jerusalem lies in heaps,
Sunken in gun metals and leads:

He sows what he reaps.
All turns upside down.
They yearn for empire: she sleeps

As an oracle. No fool or clown
Can read the numbers. He calls
Her name for the first time, her gown

Like silk spun from the stars. The halls
Of paradise are both here and afar,
Make love spring water on this last day.

XXIV

☙

Between garden and garden
This veil enshrouds us, takes
Our death sentence to weigh our burden

And leaves us for dead. What makes
Us unmakes us: we descend
And are left, we seek small stakes,

Our blood mulberry, as we end
Less than we began, and cold
To the desolation that cannot mend

Our days. This flesh once bold
Is chastened in the grave. We go
Effluent into the dark earth, old

And broken in this dream. Slow
The night that gathers us, we poison
The earth. But if love were the law

And heaven were our bones, the sun
On our faces before and after,
What might we do that hasn't been done?

XXV

☙

And what aweful thoughts go through
My foolish head, sleeping and waking,
No excuse, in the dark and blue

Of hope and despair. Not for the taking
These abstractions, the snow glows
On the distant field, the world breaking

What stories we told ourselves. Nature slows
As we slow, and the rotten plot
And underplot in head and blood grow

And grow. The mythology of being caught
Between fire and light, earth
And heaven, turns us in this waste to nought.

And we are cast out at birth
As offal in a sprawling world
Once given to plenty, now to dearth.

But on the horizon there beyond gold
Is a vision of what might be a soul
Going into paradise, not some broken wold.

XXVI

☙

And so a light as if on a coast,
A lighthouse beacon showing some way
Like a warrior who liked to boast

But could not find ground. Day
Takes us in and leaves us out
And we would like to love and play

To the end of time, but we shout,
Deaf and blind, grope for who
Knows what. We rout

Ourselves even at the gate. Do
We break our questions into simple lines
Or do we seek what is not there? Blue

Is the face from work and stress,
Stars in the east and west
But paradise is here and now.

LIGHT

I

☙

What vision of beatitude eludes
This soul, caught between more than a dilemma
So that nothing triumphs that exudes

A confidence worthy of earthly power?
I could not remember what I saw
On that road with laurel fallen away. Her

Hair was the light of reason, but no law
Could contain its scent. And the muse
Sings to Apollo between the slopes. Raw

Feelings well up, and Ovid, caught in a ruse,
Was changed to a sea-god and changed
The name of lust for ever. Who would accuse

This world of a dying light, split and ranged
Before paradise, caught in a footnote
To the universe, in human desire arranged

Limp and lame like a bad rhyme? Rote
I learn by and by: the breath of Minerva
Cannot revive the desire I lose like an old coat.

II

❃

She sat beyond the teeth of the furrows
He watched her as a way to God: thorn
And bush he bore, and she in her sorrows

Bore as some paradigm shed. Cold, borne
From a dark wood, the snow biting neck
And hand, he heard in the distance a horn

Moan like a love lost. And in the strew and wreck
He left his senses, like the errant youth
Who fell for his face in the pool. His trek,

Long and arduous, went on in search of truth
And the radiance of angels was swathed in light
While beauty sang beyond the shade. Ruth

And anxious hours awaited him. This night
Will shed its wreckage, and still ahead
A bliss will await, and terror and might

Will be gone. Through doubt, they parsed and read
Signs that obscured and were obscured
Till desire and faith were born from his head.

III

❃

She lectured him on freedom of will
Which was his idea of paradise
While empires fell, and on the hill

Of skulls he lay broken. A vice
So cruel they kept nations in terror
Crucifixion in the face of Roman law. Twice

The contradiction for the error
Adam made. In his eyes the empire
Was divine, and nothing was fairer

Than punishing the Jews. And in this fire
And holocaust, remember that Christ
Was a Jew. Ideology makes a liar

Of us all. The ovens in the mist
Make bread of our sins, leave
Us to leaven from his bleeding wrists

Our salvation. The days we bereave
Are our lost kin, the calumny
Of our skin: what we doubt, we believe.

IV

☙

Light alters over time: she could see
The mind of God: we were all punished
For that murder. And while they plea

Physics and genetics have finished
Myth off. Other myths arise. She denies
Those contra mercy and truth, to be replenished

In a world of peril. And love he decries
From the wound. The machines cart them to death-
    camps
While Goebbels becomes the master of lies.

And for that we all die. On and off-ramps
Take us here and there in this world,
Cast us broken and unburied in the damp

While at Nuremburg the banners are unfurled
And the theatre of political terror
Shakes with a rage against reason. Curled

Up is the scapegoat, the borne and the bearer,
Dead are the poets, gypsies and Jews.
Rage for the dying light, the layer

Laid in a strange dew. These small feet, large shoes
Leave us with small mercies and great truths
And nature is left in rupture with nothing to lose.

V

☙

See how mental stress tears them. Her eyes fill
With tears, his palms bleed, Rahab
And Joshua, a type of scarlet thread. Will

To power has done us in. Rehab
For all our addictions displays
Our frailty. The moon, zodiac, lab

Mix the lucent shade of our days.
The halos rot while men plot. Frozen
From Magnus to Aquinas, the doctrine delays

The eyes of God in our human gaze. Zen
Is a dream we seek like Elysium:
We kill with knives what we cannot with a pen.

God, I am done. My flesh and tongue are dumb
And matter is a mystery still, and dispute
Is everywhere around us. The sculptor's thumb

Is left in this rib of clay. Do not impute
Motives in dark and light, the moon
Is a rune on a ragged road that will not suit.

VI

☙

More light shines on them. Cherubs and seraphs
Burn and radiate, rising in the vernal
Equinox, dayspring and epigraphs

Bring in creation and the eternal
Incarnation. The poor fisherman endures
Before the order of power. The diurnal

Grind leaves us all behind, ensures
This hard and marvellous life survives
The division of our minds. What lures

Take us from ourselves, make our lives
Like dimmer rays reflected? What elect
Can there be in this shambles? These hives

We call cities make none of us select
But a swarm of rotting corpses, undone
In the weight of this sad time, wrecked

On the ruin we have made under the sun
Wrong choices, wizened fruit, long faces
Leaving for dead what the angels have done.

VII

☙

Felix costrutto, Dominus. B Nonsense.
Tags and rags quaesunt pauperum Dei
The meek shall inherit the earth hence

The ergo of irrational greed. See
How we fall from the tree, gardens
Are lost in the rearview mirror. Plea

With the rich to share: they harden
As they grow soft. The desert lies empty
As a compendium scattered on the wind. Sin

Is a burnt ember, a word at sea
With the modern world. Redemption lies
In the marketplace of souls. Even a flea

Can bring a black death. She pauses then cries
As he makes her a trope on his way
While spinning theories that will arise

In brightness and motion, make night and day
An allegory of psychomachia:
Ariadne's thread is broken and has no play.

VIII

☙

Living light, lucent source, triune radiance
These are not the coal fires of industry
But dreams of subtle shade and cadence

And in a love from the deep blue sea
Light that shines through temporal things
Ideas declining to matter. This deity

Of efficiency is not the God of love. Sing
O Heavenly Muse of the first fall
Away, the exile beyond gate and ring

That led us out to death. Recall
The errant search for truth, the tree
That bore the knowing fruit, the small

Hands held up. This is a long way to be
From glorified bodies made whole, time
A wound, invisible light made in the story

Visible. How can the eyes behold in grime
This raised light from the fire? Grace rises
And the light of love heals our first crime.

IX

☙

They blew her to bits after they shot her
How politics kills. Paradise is far off
The yoke closes on our necks: she will not stir

For her children. The wind will not scoff
At what remains: it will not brush her face
On a summer's eve. And now the whiff

Of death lies scattered in the road. Grace
Retreats like an allegory. And the cold
Days set in for us all. This great space

Closes in on us and we all grow old
In the depravity of force. I did
Not know her, and however bold

And whatever she did
She did not deserve this.
Who does? The blood stood

Lies in the road. No light can lift the smoke. Who hid
The good from us? The voice goes in a blast
And in a moment they get rid

Of peace. The garden is broken and lost
Her face, her hand, the others twisted —
Lie at angles to the fault — quake and roast.

X

☙

The light that is most beautiful shines
Ineffable, a kind of grace far from exile
And the knights at their table read signs

Of love Guinevere might muse or wile
And empires falling like drunks in the road
And the heralds are dead from bile

And the politics of greed. The poor bear their load
Leaving history by the gate. A view
Of eternity might mislead and goad

Those who seek the here and now. In lieu
Of flowers send poems and theorems
Of such elegance that they will imbue

Us with a ravishing beauty. Light dims
At the horizon, and the shadows grow
Long along the centre and the rims

We inhabit and long for. How slow
The moon rises over the ruin, the cases
Of waste and junk give off an unearthly glow.

XI

☙

This would be a history of factions
But who would care in time, whether this pope,
King, queen or president took action

Efficacious or not? But our hope
Lies with what they did or not, who said
What to whom. Time is and is not a rope

To climb or to hang on. She died in bed
After decades of rule, childless, her brain
Turning inward, her eyes, tongue, head

Heavy, her many languages at rest. The rain
May or may not have fallen. The players
Did not play for her any more. The main

Lay quiet, her parents' bodies in layers
Rested in the royal tombs. Her palace
Lay far from Rome and Florence: no soothsayers

Came as they did for Cleopatra. Bliss
Might have awaited her at the end
The Virgin Queen whom paradise might kiss.

XII

☙

What mirror could you gaze on and find
In its reflected splendour the mind of God?
Her eyes he saw eternal pleasure in kind.

The muse sang to Charlemagne at odds
With the red light of Mars. Cold Saturn
Burned white, glowing circles and rods

Remnants of the Big Bang. The worlds turn
Until empires fall and eagles die
Till the head of the Baptist will return

And be made whole from a fractured lie.
And atonement will come. Justice will arise
Amid nuclear waste and the blood and dye

Of war rubble. Amid whispers and cries
The full light of divine grace shines on him
A laser that peals away his pride and lies

Like cataracts. What first light a limb
Shaped the universe? Dark ignorance
Is hard to dispel in a world so dim.

XIII

☙

Beware science and theology made
Politics, the division of the kingdom
His crown thorns, his bones broken like sticks

And baptism and scientific method, and some
Other hopes worked against inexorable time.
The abuses in churches and schools make us dumb

In the eloquence of nature. These bones are lime
In the lye. The prince of peace rises high
After a time, breaking time

In half a line, by
And by, half the time. The glorified
Body comes unbroken with a sigh.

A bridge of sighs. No more drawn or denied,
He blinds him, the mystical rose
At his side: he cannot be judged or tried

Any more. And John also blinds him. Her clothes
Are gossamer to recognition
He sees again, and on his face the wind blows.

XIV

☙

Love from Alpha to Omega, reason, scripture
Experiment and metaphor make a stab
At the gap, wound, hole, rupture

Left in us, in nature. This world is our lab
And we cannot be sure. What we see
In our way. Love is good. Queen Mab

Is the nano of the cosmos. The Holy See
Peter denounced for decline, which led
To further division. Pope Lear cannot flee

His daughters. Uncivil wars have bred
Such barbarity that the moon is blood
Fire amid the mid-winter snow. The red

Stains stars and soil. And by the broken rood
She stands, her eyes a mirror of light
Her cries rainbows. And the rude

History of nails and spears breaks in.
Flight, fright, fight all make an awful rhyme
While sparks from the heavens alight.

XV

☙

The frost came, the pollen went, time still stuns
Flesh, eyes, bones, mind, soul: in eternity
There is no before and after: roses and guns

Make and unmake us. For some, in this sea
There is no end of time. Others say
Time never began before creation: a plea

For evolution comes late but stays
With us. Form and matter become, puzzle
The will: angels cause debates and frays

Among theologians. And dreams are muzzles
And angels live in the present, and winter
Is almost come. The war in heaven, the fizzles

Of the one bearing pride in light, falls out,
Goes on: the acid smoke of evil drizzles
As if a comic line. No nostalgia for the rout

Of Roman or barbarian.
And mercy came, dry air and light
Without vortex or spout.

XVI

☙

A rose is a rose, a rose can be sick
Burn in holy fire, through light till desire
Was consumed. And in this flame a wick

Burnt without consumption and the fire
Came from a grace no words could express
And the light was alive, a choir

Sang rainbows from light,
The prisms Newton saw, and the poet
Became one in a vision of beatific bliss.

XVII

☙

And what might end in this flux?
Can we feel in the face of oblivion?
Hard by the docks and stews fiat lux

Is good news. And in this terrible mess
Of efflux and effluent we stumble blind
In a world where we can only assert and guess.

The scaffold of ideas comes and goes, rind
Mistaken for pith at the time. The stream
Curtains over the smooth rocks lined

And shaded even in the winter sun. The ream
Of spring is about to break, scatter pollen
On the breeze, bees abuzz, heat and beam

Melting my marrow. And in the spin
Of the wind a green garden grows, peers
Through the blooming trees. The sin

Is not to try to know, love being wise, ears
Open to earth and sky. The quick and the dead:
As an act of love we chase away our fears.

XVIII

☙

She was as the moon on a winter's night
The snowdrifts gathered on her steps
And her face was a gracious light

To young eyes. We love here and now, maps
Of eternity, and fold when spring
Is almost come. She comes. Time rips

This flesh. Whoever we are, sprung
From flesh, we are harvested, gone
Before we know it. How, so spent and wrung,

Can we heal ourselves, mend the world
For ever, make ourselves whole? And then
I turn back to her as if she were the dawn,

The next light to waken us from the dark
And keep us from being dupes and pawns.
In the alley the wind blows, the dogs bark.

XIX

☙

And paradise cannot be
An anticlimax on a rough sea
The music of the spheres awry

In the static of an angry sky
Rhyme's reason deafens
As time lessens and lessens

Quite a lesson. Paradise
Cannot be a vice, advice,
A vise, not trivial

The Tigris and Euphrates fluvial
Irregular and modern
Whatever that means. The fern

Obscures what demurs: perne
Adam and Eve in a gyre
Burnt in Yeats' holy fire

And Dante speaks of the rose
No vision of a garden hose.
This comedy is no laughing matter

Matter cannot laugh: the Mad Hatter
Moves from order through disorder
To order: paradise knows no borders.

XX

❧

How soon has time, that's a good line
About being the subtle thief of youth
There's some truth that we can't define

In poetry, something satire and spoof
Can't quite catch. That leaves poets,
Like mathematicians, elegant and aloof.

But what has this to do with fêtes
And paradise, light after the bets
Lost to fire? Paradise is not a lame

Run-on rhyme. The dying of the light
Is no gentle thing for those who doubt.
The half-rhyme of these eyes

Leads to the half-line of our demise.
God have mercy on our souls. The first cause
Cannot judge except by its logic and laws

Reason and faith, science and humanities
Can they work together without inanities?
The sun is warm on his old face

And he hopes for the good grace
Of life ever after, no illusion or myth
Or simply another figure with a scythe?

XXI

☙

We are of our time, blind before the future,
The thought of death a deadly rupture
A nausea tempting suicide,

Nothing to paper over or elide,
Something hard to elude: Our mortal coil
Shuffles us off before we know it

As if we are torn bit by bit
And look for what we can say and do
To confront ourselves and others, blue

On a sea of trouble. You don't need
To be a Danish prince to think of being
And non-being, here and hereafter, seeing

What we can of this seeming world. She drowned
In rue for remembrance. Even the clowns
Die, alas. And what jests and laughter

Can ward against dire time and disaster?
May flights of angels carry us all
To a paradise beyond pale and pall.

NOTES

"rust" ('Fire', IV): The rust is an echo of the rust and moth in the Bible: "But lay up for yourselves treasures in heaven, where neither moth nor rust doth corrupt, and where thieves do not break through nor steal." (Matthew 6:20)

"perse" ('Fire', V): A dark blue, bluish-grey or purplish-black colour.

"Features, the tongues rump and roll" ('Fire', XI): "Rump" is here used as a verb in an innovative comic sense sounding like a rump; NOT, "to have sexual intercourse".

"yard" ('Fire', XIII): As in the early and North American usage, meaning garden plot of earth; metaphorical for land.

"furniture" ('Fire', XIV): Literally and figuratively, the weight of possessions, stealing a soul despite the seeming permanence of furniture or possessions.

"Sinon" ('Fire', XIX): Sinon was the Greek who persuaded the Trojans to bring the wooden horse into Troy (Virgil *Æneid* ii. 57 sqq.).

"rise and fall" ('Between', IV): It is left to the reader to fill in specifics (such as, the wheel of fortune, empires etc.).

"the last mile" ('Between', IV): Metaphorical reference to the Last Judgement.

"Looked back, here and before" ('Between', XXI): Place and time are deliberately mixed.

"what beckoned, belied" ('Between', XXII): Something beckons but also deceives (oxymoron).

"perne" ('Light', XIX): "Spin / revolve". Echo of Yeats' poem, 'Sailing to Byzantium'.

THE INTERNATIONAL PROVERSE POETRY PRIZE (SINGLE POEMS)

An annual international Proverse Poetry Prize (for single poems) was established in 2016. The international Proverse Poetry Prize is open to all who are at least eighteen years old whatever their residence, nationality or citizenship.

Single poems, submitted in English, are invited on (a) <u>any subject or theme, chosen by the writer</u> OR (b) <u>on a subject or theme selected by the organizers each year</u>.

Poems may be in any form, style or genre. Each poem should be no more than 30 lines.

Entries should previously be unpublished in any way (except in the case of unpublished translations into English of the entrant's own work already published in another language, providing the entrant holds the copyright).

**In 2016, cash prizes were offered as follows:
1st prize; USD100.00; 2nd prize: USD45.00;
3rd prizes (up to four winners): USD20.00.**

KEY DATES FOR THE PROVERSE POETRY PRIZE IN 2017 ONWARDS
(subject to confirmation and/or change)

Receipt of entered work, entry forms and entry fees	7 May to 14 July of the year of entry
Announcement of Winners	Before April of the year following the year of entry
Cash Awards Made	At the same time as publication of the winning poems (whether in the Proverse newsletter or website, or in an anthology)
Publication of an anthology of winning and other selected entries	Contingent on the quality of entries in any year

The above information is for guidance only. More information, updated from time to time, is available on the Proverse website: proversepublishing.com

POETRY AND POETRY COLLECTIONS
Published by Proverse Hong Kong

Astra and Sebastian, by L.W. Illsley. 2011.
Chasing light, by Patricia Glinton Meicholas. 2013.
China suite and other poems, by Gillian Bickley. 2009.
For the record and other poems of Hong Kong,
    by Gillian Bickley. 2003.
Frida Kahlo's Cry and Other Poems,
    by Laura Solomon. 2015.
Home, away, elsewhere, by Vaughan Rapatahana. 2011.
Immortelle and bhandaaraa poems,
    by Lelawattee Manoo-Rahming. 2011.
In vitro, by Laura Solomon. 2nd ed. 2014.
Irreverent Poems for Pretentious People,
    by Henrik Hoeg. 2016.
Moving house and other poems from Hong Kong,
    by Gillian Bickley. 2005.
Of Leaves & Ashes, by Patty Ho. 2016.
Of symbols misused, by Mary-Jane Newton. 2011.
Painting the borrowed house: poems,
    by Kate Rogers. 2008.
Perceptions, by Gillian Bickley. 2012.
Rain on the pacific coast, by Elbert Siu Ping Lee. 2013.
refrain, by Jason S. Polley. 2010.
Shadow play, by James Norcliffe. 2012.
Shadows in Deferment, by Birgit Bunzel Linder. 2013.
Shifting Sands, by Deepa Vanjani. 2016.
Sightings: a collection of poetry, with an essay, 'communicating poems', by Gillian Bickley. 2007.
Smoked pearl: poems of Hong Kong and beyond,
    by Akin Jeje (Akinsola Olufemi Jeje). 2010.
The Layers Between (Essays and Poems),
    by Celia Claase. 2015.
Unlocking, by Mary-Jane Newton. March 2014.
Wonder, lust & itchy feet, by Sally Dellow. 2011.

FIND OUT MORE ABOUT OUR AUTHORS BOOKS, EVENTS AND LITERARY PRIZES

Visit our website:
http://www.proversepublishing.com

Visit our distributor's website: <www.chineseupress.com>

Follow us on Twitter
Follow news and conversation: twitter.com/proversebooks>
OR
Copy and paste the following to your browser window and follow the instructions:
https://twitter.com/#!/ProverseBooks
"Like" us on www.facebook.com/ProversePress

Request our free E-Newsletter
Send your request to info@proversepublishing.com.

Availability
Most titles are available in Hong Kong and world-wide from our Hong Kong based Distributor,
The Chinese University of Hong Kong Press,
The Chinese University of Hong Kong, Shatin, NT, Hong Kong SAR, China.
Email: cup-bus@cuhk.edu.hk
Website: <www.chineseupress.com>.
All titles are available from Proverse Hong Kong
http://www.proversepublishing.com
and the Proverse Hong Kong UK-based Distributor.

We have **stock-holding retailers** in Hong Kong,
Singapore (Select Books),
Canada (Elizabeth Campbell Books),
Andorra (Llibreria La Puça, La Llibreria).
Orders can be made from bookshops in the UK and elsewhere.

Ebooks
Most of our titles are available also as Ebooks.

www.ingramcontent.com/pod-product-compliance
Lightning Source LLC
Chambersburg PA
CBHW051133160426
43195CB00014B/2452